GRAPHIC EXPEDITIONS

ESCAPE FROM
POMPEII

AN *Isabel Soto*
ARCHAEOLOGY ADVENTURE

by Terry Collins

illustrated by Cynthia Martin and Barbara Schulz

Consultant:
Richard S. Williams
Associate Professor of History
Washington State University

CAPSTONE PRESS
a capstone imprint

Graphic Library is published by Capstone Press,
151 Good Counsel Drive, P.O. Box 669, Mankato, Minnesota 56002.
www.capstonepub.com

092011
006366R

Library of Congress Cataloging-in-Publication Data
Collins, Terry.
    Escape from Pompeii : an Isabel Soto archaeology adventure / by Terry Collins;
illustrated by Cynthia Martin and Barbara Schulz.
    p. cm.—(Graphic library. Graphic expeditions)
    Summary: "In graphic novel format, follows the adventures of Isabel Soto as she
explores the ancient city of Pompeii"—Provided by publisher.
    Includes bibliographical references and index.
    ISBN 978-1-4296-4771-7 (library binding)
    ISBN 978-1-4296-5634-4 (paperback)
    1. Pompeii (Extinct city)—Comic books, strips, etc.—Juvenile literature. 2. Graphic
novels—Juvenile literature. I. Martin, Cynthia, 1961– ill. II. Schulz, Barbara (Barbara Jo), ill.
III. Title. IV. Series.
DG70.P7C624 2011
937'.7256807—dc22   2010007245

Designer
Alison Thiele

Media Researcher
Wanda Winch

Cover Artist
Tod G. Smith

Production Specialist
Laura Manthe

Colorist
Krista Ward

Editors
Aaron Sautter and Marissa Bolte

Photo credits: iStockphoto/Tatiana Belova, 7; Shutterstock/Andrea Danti, 23;
    Shutterstock/Naaman Abreu, 14; Wikipedia/John Reinhardt, B24 tailgunner,
    USAAF, WWII, 21;

Design elements: Shutterstock/Chen Ping Hung (framed edge design); mmmm (world
    map design); Mushakesa (abstract lines design); Najin (old parchment design)

TABLE OF CONTENTS

I'm Dr. Antonio Giordano. I work here at the Pompeii ruins. I'm showing Ms. Mancini around. Would you like to join us?

Gladly! I'd love to explore one of the world's most famous archaeological sites.

These ruins are so quiet. It's hard to believe that Pompeii was once a busy city filled with people.

Yes. That all ended when Mount Vesuvius erupted on August 24, AD 79.

ACTIVE OR NOT?

Mount Vesuvius was last active in 1944. Although it has not erupted for more than 60 years, the volcano is not dormant. Scientists believe the volcano will erupt again in the future.

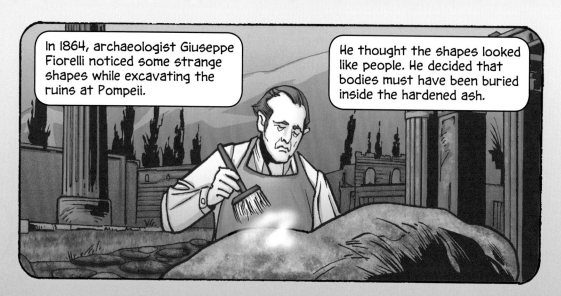

In 1864, archaeologist Giuseppe Fiorelli noticed some strange shapes while excavating the ruins at Pompeii.

He thought the shapes looked like people. He decided that bodies must have been buried inside the hardened ash.

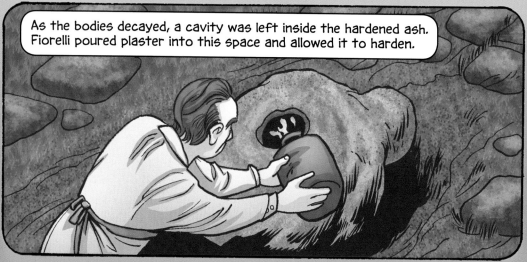

As the bodies decayed, a cavity was left inside the hardened ash. Fiorelli poured plaster into this space and allowed it to harden.

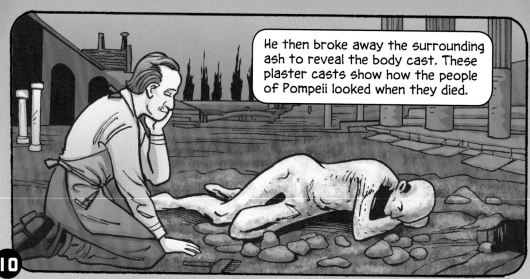

He then broke away the surrounding ash to reveal the body cast. These plaster casts show how the people of Pompeii looked when they died.

Pompeii, Italy, February 5, AD 62

There you are!
Are you okay?

I—I think so. This is amazing, Isabel!
I can't believe I'm seeing ancient
Pompeii with my own eyes.

This must be the Sarno Gate.
It was the main entrance into
Pompeii, right?

That's right. According to the W.I.S.P.,
the wall is 26 feet, or 8 meters, high
and 20 feet, or 6 meters, thick. There
are also 12 lookout towers.

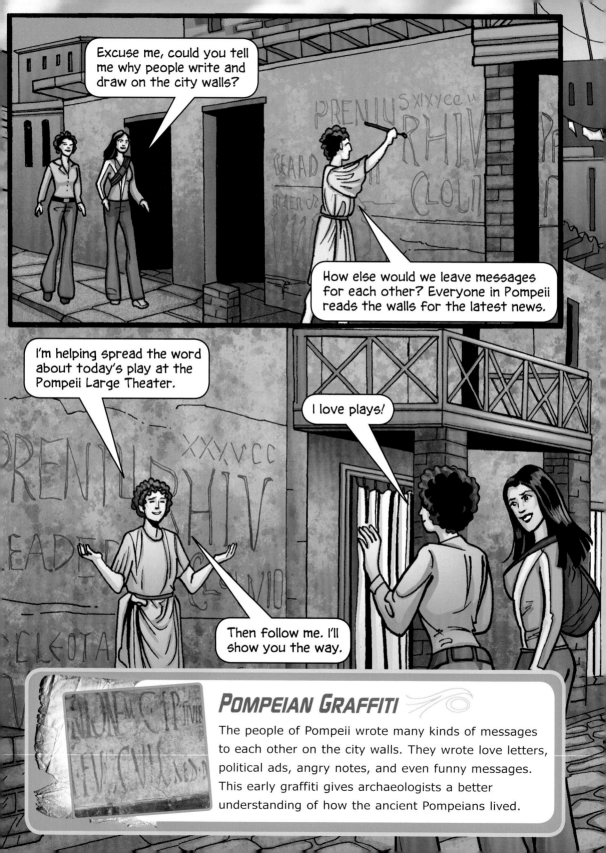

Pompeian Graffiti

The people of Pompeii wrote many kinds of messages to each other on the city walls. They wrote love letters, political ads, angry notes, and even funny messages. This early graffiti gives archaeologists a better understanding of how the ancient Pompeians lived.

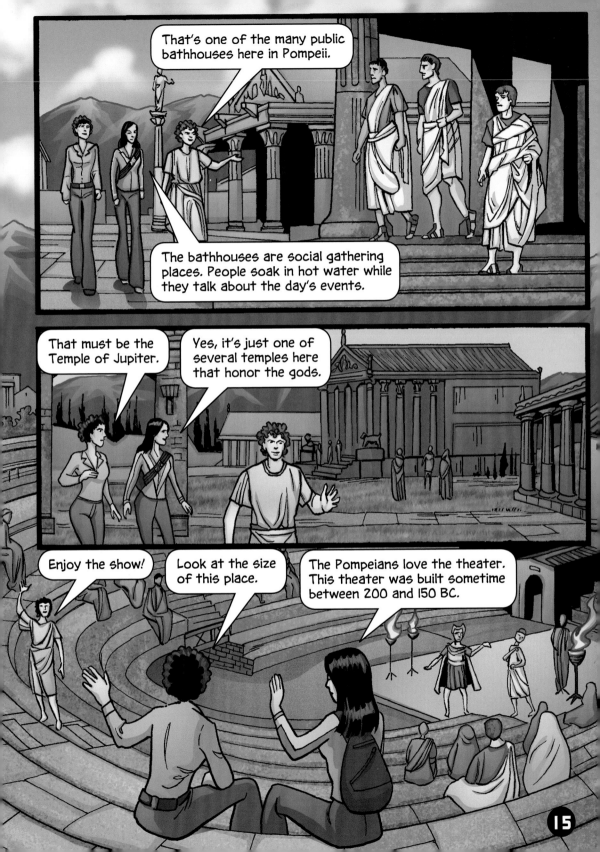

19

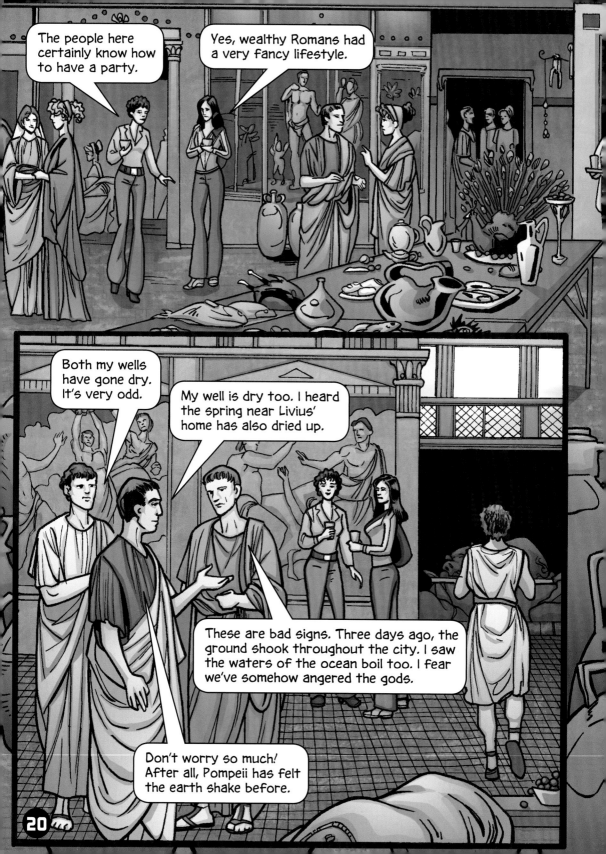

TERRIBLE TREMORS

Several strong tremors served as early warning signs before Mount Vesuvius erupted. While some people in Pompeii chose to ignore the signs, most decided to flee the city until things calmed down. Only a few thousand people were in Pompeii when Mount Vesuvius erupted.

KRAKADOOOOMM!!

THE ERUPTION

The eruption lasted for more than 24 hours. A cloud of hot ash, rocks, and gas, called a pyroclastic surge, came around midnight. That first surge covered the city with 3 feet, or 0.9 meters, of pumice. Eleven more surges completely buried Pompeii.

25

Pompeii, Italy, present day

There you are!
I was so worried!

Dr. Giordano, we saw
Mount Vesuvius erupt!

Your accidental trip may
turn out to be a good thing.
Now you can write about
what Pompeii was really like.

I could also point out how
important it is to preserve
what's left of Pompeii.

Maybe your story will help
increase our funding. We
have much work left to do!

MORE ABOUT POMPEII

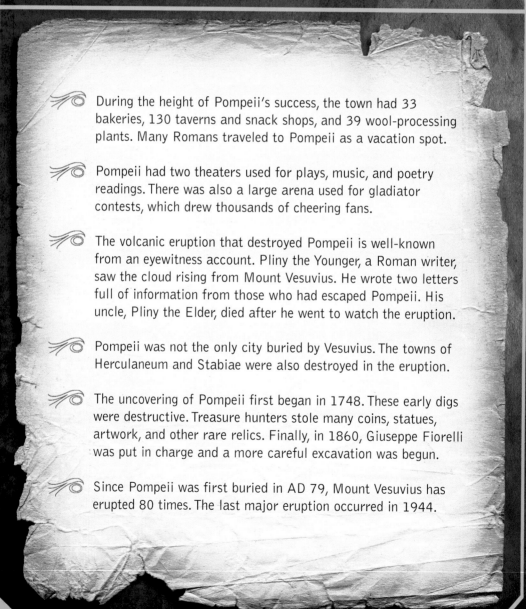

- During the height of Pompeii's success, the town had 33 bakeries, 130 taverns and snack shops, and 39 wool-processing plants. Many Romans traveled to Pompeii as a vacation spot.

- Pompeii had two theaters used for plays, music, and poetry readings. There was also a large arena used for gladiator contests, which drew thousands of cheering fans.

- The volcanic eruption that destroyed Pompeii is well-known from an eyewitness account. Pliny the Younger, a Roman writer, saw the cloud rising from Mount Vesuvius. He wrote two letters full of information from those who had escaped Pompeii. His uncle, Pliny the Elder, died after he went to watch the eruption.

- Pompeii was not the only city buried by Vesuvius. The towns of Herculaneum and Stabiae were also destroyed in the eruption.

- The uncovering of Pompeii first began in 1748. These early digs were destructive. Treasure hunters stole many coins, statues, artwork, and other rare relics. Finally, in 1860, Giuseppe Fiorelli was put in charge and a more careful excavation was begun.

- Since Pompeii was first buried in AD 79, Mount Vesuvius has erupted 80 times. The last major eruption occurred in 1944.

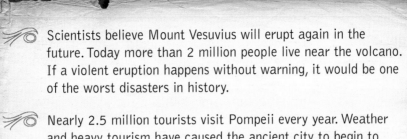

Scientists believe Mount Vesuvius will erupt again in the future. Today more than 2 million people live near the volcano. If a violent eruption happens without warning, it would be one of the worst disasters in history.

Nearly 2.5 million tourists visit Pompeii every year. Weather and heavy tourism have caused the ancient city to begin to crumble. Artwork on the walls has also faded badly. In 2008, the Italian government declared a state of emergency to help restore and preserve the ancient ruins at Pompeii.

MORE ABOUT

Isabel Soto

NAME: Dr. Isabel "Izzy" Soto
DEGREES: History and Anthropology
BUILD: Athletic **HAIR:** Dark Brown
EYES: Brown **HEIGHT:** 5' 7"

W.I.S.P.: The Worldwide Inter-dimensional Space/Time Portal developed by Max Axiom at Axiom Laboratory.

BACKSTORY: Dr. Isabel "Izzy" Soto caught the history bug as a little girl. Every night, her grandfather told her about his adventures exploring ancient ruins in South America. He believed lost cultures teach people a great deal about history.

Izzy's love of cultures followed her to college. She studied history and anthropology. On a research trip to Thailand, she discovered an ancient stone with mysterious energy. Izzy took the stone to Super Scientist Max Axiom who determined that the stone's energy cuts across space and time. Harnessing the power of the stone, he built a device called the W.I.S.P. It opens windows to any place and any time. Izzy now travels through time to see history unfold before her eyes. Although she must not change history, she can observe and investigate historical events.

GLOSSARY

archaeologist (ar-kee-AH-luh-jist)—a scientist who studies how people lived in the past

cast (KAST)—a model of an object in plaster; casts show details of the original object

cavity (KA-vuh-tee)—a hole or hollow space

dormant (DOR-muhnt)—not active; dormant volcanoes have not erupted for many years

excavate (EK-skuh-vayt)—to dig in the earth

gladiator (GLAD-ee-ay-tur)—an ancient Roman slave who fought against other gladiators or fierce animals to entertain the public

graffiti (gruh-FEE-tee)—pictures drawn or words written on the walls of buildings or other surfaces

preserve (pree-ZURV)—to protect something so it stays in its original form

pumice (PUHM-iss)—a light, grayish volcanic rock

pyroclastic surge (PYE-roh-KLAS-tic SURJ)—a cloud of hot ash, rocks, and gas

relic (REL-ik)—something that has survived from the past

ruins (ROO-ins)—the remains of a building or other things that have fallen down or been destroyed

tremor (TREM-ur)—a shaking or trembling movement

tribute (TRIB-yoot)—gifts given to the gods to show respect

villa (VIL-uh)—a large, fancy house, especially one in the country

READ MORE

Harbo, Christopher L. *The Explosive World of Volcanoes with Max Axiom, Super Scientist.* Graphic Science. Mankato, Minn.: Capstone Press, 2008.

Lindeen, Mary. *Ashes to Ashes: Uncovering Pompeii.* Shockwave. New York: Children's Press, 2008.

Malam, John. *You Wouldn't Want to Live in Pompeii!: A Volcanic Eruption You'd Rather Avoid.* New York: Franklin Watts, 2008.

Samuel, Charlie. *Solving the Mysteries of Pompeii.* Digging into History. Tarrytown, N.Y.: Marshall Cavendish Benchmark, 2009.

INTERNET SITES

FactHound offers a safe, fun way to find Internet sites related to this book. All sites on FactHound have been researched by our staff.

Here's all you do:

Visit *www.facthound.com*

Type in this code: 9781429647717